CLARK: The Velcro Dog Who Stuck to My Heart

A Memoir by Adam Lee Meade

Clark: The Velcro Dog Who Stuck to My Heart
© 2025 **Adam Lee Meade**

Publisher:
Adam Lee Meade Publishing
18 Deer View Court Fayetteville, West Virginia, USA

ISBN (Paperback): 979-8-9937801-0-8

ISBN (Hardback): 979-8-9937801-2-2

ISBN (eBook): 979-8-9937801-1-5

Cover Design: Adam Meade

Interior Design: Adam Meade

This is a work of nonfiction. Some names, locations, and identifying details may have been changed to protect the privacy of individuals. Every effort has been made to accurately represent events as they occurred.

Publisher's Note:
This book reflects the personal experiences, memories, and interpretations of the author. The publisher and author assume no responsibility for errors or omissions, or for the interpretation of the information contained herein.

For Clark — my best friend.

Table of Contents

Prologue: A Pawprint on My Heart

Some dogs drift quietly into your life. Clark didn't. He charged in—tail wagging, eyes bright, Doberman confidence wrapped around a heart that somehow already belonged to me.

I still remember the first time I held him—a six-week-old red rust puppy with oversized paws and a spirit that filled the room. I thought I was getting a dog. What I didn't realize was that I was gaining a compass—someone who would quietly guide me through both the darkest nights and the brightest days of my life.

Back then, my world wasn't tidy. I was navigating life changes—work, relationships, and figuring out who I was supposed to be in my early thirties. There were more questions than answers, more noise than peace. But Clark didn't care about any of that. He just knew I was his person. And from the moment he looked at me, that was enough.

The early days were a mix of chaos and laughter—sloppy kisses, endless games of fetch or frisbee, and that classic Doberman whine that could melt your patience and your heart at the same time. But underneath the puppy energy was a kind of wisdom. When Clark looked at me, it wasn't the look of a pet waiting for direction—it was something closer to understanding.

He had a way of simplifying life. To Clark, things were beautifully straightforward: play hard, love harder, protect what matters. He could turn a stick into treasure, a walk into an adventure, and a quiet evening into something sacred.

Over time, we built our own language. We didn't need words. When life got heavy, he was always there—steady, watchful, grounding. In tune with my every emotion. He didn't fix anything. He just was. And somehow, that was everything.

Looking back, I see that Clark's story wasn't just about a dog. It was about loyalty, resilience, and a love that doesn't fade— the kind that changes you, and stays long after the pawprints on the floor have disappeared.

This isn't just his story.

It's ours.

Chapter One: The Doberman

The decision to get a Doberman wasn't made lightly. I explored many breeds, searching for one that was low maintenance and fit my active lifestyle. After careful thought, I focused on Dobermans. I'd always admired the breed—regal, athletic, fiercely loyal—but didn't fully grasp what living with one really meant. I read what owners said, but nothing truly prepares you until you have one. One thing was certain: I needed something solid to keep me grounded amid the chaos.

So, one evening, sitting alone with my thoughts, I posted a simple message on Facebook: "Anyone know of any Doberman litters around?" Within hours, a friend messaged me about a family in Bluefield, West Virginia. They had a litter just a few days old. Without hesitation, I called. They told me I could come the next weekend.

When I pulled into their driveway, the mountain air felt charged with anticipation. The house sat tucked between trees, immaculate. The lawn and field were perfectly striped, warmth apparent from the outside. A woman greeted me at the door, asked me to remove my shoes and wash my hands. I thought, 'These are people who care.'

She led me into the garage. I wasn't ready. The space was now a spotless nursery. Blankets lined the floor; the air, climate-controlled, faintly smelled of apple pie and wood shavings. Then came the sound—tiny whimpers, squeaks, like living wind chimes.

Doberman puppies tumbled over one another, a storm of black and rust-colored fur, each one trying to out-wiggle the next. I crouched down, my knees cracking as I tried to take in the moment. I reached out a hand, not sure which one to touch first. And that's when it happened. From the pile, one little pup pulled himself free. He wasn't the biggest or the loudest. In fact, he seemed almost unsure—his paws too big for his body, his ears flopping as he stumbled forward. But his eyes locked onto mine, steady and certain, and he climbed right into my lap.

There was no hesitation, no second-guessing. He curled against me, sighed, and that was it. He'd chosen me. The breeder smiled, watching quietly. "Looks like he knows where he's supposed to be," she said.

And I think she was right.

I held him longer than I should have, feeling his heartbeat against my chest. He smelled like warmth and innocence, his puppy breath melting me. I didn't say it aloud, but I knew I held a new beginning.

Before I left, I paid the deposit and filled out the paperwork. The breeder told me I could take him home when he turned eight weeks old. As I stood there looking back at the litter, that one pup—my pup—watched me leave with those same steady eyes, as if to say, Don't worry. I'll be here when you come back.

Driving home, I couldn't stop thinking about him. I tried out names in my head. Only one stuck—Clark. It fit. Strong but gentle. Noble without trying. Like Clark Kent—ordinary on the surface, but extraordinary underneath.

I didn't know it yet, but Clark wasn't just going to be part of my life—he was about to change it.

Bringing Him Home

The day I brought Clark home, the weather was relentless. It had rained for almost two weeks straight—gray skies, misty mornings, and that steady Appalachian drizzle that seeps into everything. The roads shimmered with puddles as I drove, windshield wipers setting a slow rhythm. Clark sat beside me, watching the world blur past. He didn't cry, didn't fuss. Just watched. Calm, curious, and—already—trusting.

By the time we arrived, the rain eased to a drizzle. I carried him in, toweled his red rust coat, and set him in the living room. Under dim light, his coloring glowed like copper against the stormy sky. He shook, gave me a look, and decided wet grass was not for him. That week of rain shaped him. From then, he avoided getting wet—a lifelong quirk.

That first night, I tried to be disciplined. I laid a soft blanket beside my bed, convinced he'd be fine sleeping there. He disagreed. Within minutes, he was whining in that classic

Doberman tone—a cross between a whimper and a rusty violin. Then came what I would come to call his horn—a drawn-out, dramatic, half-howl that started deep in his chest and climbed until it sounded almost like a foghorn. It was funny, cute, and maddening all at once.

I caved. He ended up in bed with me, curled tight against my chest, that tiny red rust body radiating more warmth than seemed possible. I told myself it was just for the night, but when dawn came and I opened my eyes to see him snoring softly beside me, I knew I was in trouble.

Still, I didn't want to start a lifelong habit, so I devised a compromise. Each night after that, I'd let him fall asleep beside me, then carefully lift him and sneak him into his crate. I'd lie there half-in, half-out of the crate, one arm draped inside so he could feel me there. When his breathing slowed and the whining stopped, I'd ease my hand away, slide the door shut, and tiptoe back to bed like a thief in my own house.

The schedule worked, mostly. I set alarms through the night, taking him out every couple of hours, rain or not. The sound of the rain on the roof became our soundtrack—steady, patient, testing our resolve. Each time I opened the door, he'd look at me like, You cannot be serious. He'd tiptoe to the edge of the overhang, hesitate, then make a mad dash into the wet grass, do his business, and sprint back under cover, shaking like he'd just escaped a hurricane.

Despite the weather, he was remarkably easy to train. He seemed to want to understand, to do things right. He had very few accidents in the house, almost none, and I could see the pride in him when he got it right—nub of a tail wagging, chest out, the faintest glimmer of "good boy" in his eyes. Even as a puppy, Clark carried himself with this odd mix of grace and seriousness, as if he already knew who he was supposed to be.

That rain-soaked start became a defining piece of him. For the rest of his life, the moment a drop hit his head, he'd freeze and glare at the sky like it had personally offended him. He'd stand under the porch, calculating if the trip to the yard was truly worth it. I'd laugh, call him dramatic, and he'd give me a look equal parts stubborn and resigned—like he knew exactly what needed to be done but wasn't thrilled about it.

Those early nights were exhausting, but I didn't mind. There was something healing in the routine—the sound of his soft snores, the warmth of his fur, the simple act of caring for something other than myself. The world outside might have been soaked and uncertain, but inside that little camper, where we lived the first six months of his life—with the rain pattering on the roof and Clark tucked beside me—it felt like peace.

Learning Each Other

By the second week, Clark had already started to show who he was going to be—a mix of sharp intelligence, stubborn pride, and comic-level drama. He wasn't the kind of dog who just followed orders; he wanted to understand the why behind them. And if he didn't agree with my reasoning, well, he had no problem negotiating.

Training him was part strategy, part stand-up comedy. The Doberman breed is famous for its intelligence, but what most people don't tell you is that they're equally skilled in manipulation. Clark figured out early that I was a soft touch. If he didn't want to do something, he'd start with the Doberman whine—that long, theatrical moan that somehow conveyed boredom, disappointment, and heartbreak all at once. If that didn't work, he'd break out his signature move: the horn.

The horn wasn't just a sound—it was a performance. It started as a low hum, a vibrating growl that rolled up through his throat until it bloomed into this long, echoing howl that could make the neighbors think I was hiding a moose in the camper. I'd tell him "enough," and he'd pause, stare me dead in the eyes, and let out one last, soft grumble, just to prove his point. He would do anything to try to get your attention and be close to you. I recall one night, as I was watching TV in my recliner, he was trying to sleep on the couch behind me but wanted to be on my lap. He eventually leaped over and landed on the top back of the recliner, knocking him and I straight back on the ground.

As frustrating as it could be, it was impossible not to laugh. The horn became his trademark. Every emotion—hunger, impatience, joy, boredom—came out in some version of that ridiculous sound. And somehow, it made the place feel alive.

He was whip-smart, too. It didn't take long for him to learn commands like "sit," "stay," and "leave it." But if he decided a task was beneath him, he'd sit there with that proud, chest-out stance and look at me as if to say, You've got to be kidding me. Sometimes I'd swear he understood sarcasm.

We also had a routine. We would get up early during my workday, do our morning rituals, then load up in the car. He'd get dropped off at his Aunt Hollie's house for doggie daycare until I picked him up after work. He loved his Aunt Hollie. He found safety and love nestled under her desk while she worked from home. She gave him the affection he needed while I was away. And he played hard with Chyna, my sister's dog. She basically showed him the ropes on how to be a dog.

Of course, not every day went smoothly. He absolutely loved to chew on my niece's stuffed animals. Toys didn't last him very long at all. One day, I came home to find Clark having trouble holding food down—ears back, head low, and a suspicious look as if he already knew, despite my stress, what he had done. Turned out he'd eaten part of a stuffed animal and, for reasons I'll never understand, a Breathe Right nasal strip. I don't think either of us slept that night. The next morning, he was at the vet, looking at me with those eyes that said, please don't be mad! Thankfully, he came out fine, but that incident set a new household rule: Clark-proof everything.

Even as a puppy, he had the confidence of a full-grown Doberman. When we'd go for walks, he'd trot beside me like he was on patrol—head high, chest forward, ears up like he owned the world. But the moment a raindrop hit his head, all that bravado disappeared. He'd stop in his tracks, look at me, then at the sky, as if questioning my leadership. You're supposed to protect me from this, his eyes seemed to say.

Our days settled into a rhythm. I'd get up before sunrise, make coffee, and open the camper door to the smell of fresh air. Clark would stretch, yawn, and step outside like a lion surveying his kingdom. Then came breakfast, a quick play session, and—of course—his morning zoomies, where he'd sprint in wide circles around the yard until his paws kicked up dirt. He'd stop suddenly, look up at me with that proud grin, and let out a little grunt like he'd just conquered something important.

We were learning from each other. I was figuring out how to lead with patience, and he was figuring out how to live in a world full of rules that didn't always make sense to him. But underneath the growing pains, something deeper was forming—a mutual understanding that we were building a life together. Every bark, every horn, every muddy pawprint on the floor was part of a language only we spoke.

Clark was still just a puppy, but already, he was teaching me something about loyalty—and about laughter. The kind that sneaks up on you after a hard day, the kind that reminds you that life's best moments are rarely the quiet ones.

Finding Peace by the River

By midsummer, the rain had finally given up its hold on the hills. The mornings turned warm and golden, and the smell of damp pine faded into the clean scent of sunlight on wet grass. The world felt new again—washed, quiet, alive.

The New River was our place.

Every evening after work, I'd grab Clark's leash, and his entire body would light up. His nub of a tail would whip in tight circles, his paws prancing as if the word walk was the best sound in the world. We'd head down a trail, where the ground softened under our boots and paws. The path wound through a tunnel of rhododendron and opened up to the New River, wide and steady, its surface catching the last light of the day.

Clark loved hiking. He'd race ahead, then turn to make sure I was following—ears perked, eyes bright, that red rust coat glowing like polished copper in the evening sun. Sometimes he'd find a stick twice his size and drag it proudly through the grass, stumbling and tripping but never giving up. Other times he'd splash into the shallows, snapping at ripples and daring the water to fight back. I'd sit on a rock nearby, boots off, letting the cool current roll past my feet, and just watch him be free.

Those evenings by the river became our rhythm. No matter how rough my day had been, Clark had a way of resetting everything. His joy was contagious. Watching him run, ears flapping and tail cutting through the air, felt like watching life itself—simple, unfiltered, unapologetically happy.

He'd always come back eventually, panting and dirty, and drop his stick at my feet like an offering. Never having to move a step, I'd reach down, ruffle the fur on his head, and he'd press against my leg, leaning in just enough to say thanks and give it a big toss.

It was in those quiet moments that I started to feel something shift. The noise in my head—the worry, the heartbreak, the endless what-ifs—faded a little each day. Clark didn't fix anything; he didn't have to. He just existed beside me with this unwavering calm, and somehow, that was enough. He reminded me what still mattered. The world had gone sideways for a while, but with him there, I could feel it steadying again.

He was growing fast, too. His legs shot up before the rest of him caught up, and for a few weeks he looked like a gangly teenager—half legs, half ears, all attitude. But even then, there was a grace in him. His stride was confident, his presence magnetic. He didn't just walk into a room—he owned it.

Sometimes I'd sit by the river in my hammock as the sun slipped below the ridge, Clark stretched out beside me, his head resting on my boots. The sound of the water and the rhythm of his breathing became the soundtrack to something I hadn't felt in a long time—peace and unconditional love.

He didn't know it, but he'd pulled me back to life.

Foreshadowing the Journey Ahead

As that first year rolled on, life began to feel a little less like something to survive and more like something to look forward to. Clark had grown from a clumsy puppy into a striking young Doberman, his red rust coat gleaming in the sunlight, his chest broad and proud. People would stop and stare when we walked by, but to me, he was still the same wide-eyed pup who'd crawled into my lap that day in Bluefield.

He'd become more than just company—he was my shadow, my alarm clock, my peacekeeper. Every part of my day revolved around him. Mornings started with his nose pressed against my face and ended with the thump of his tail against the floor as I got ready for bed. I didn't go anywhere without him, and honestly, I didn't want to. The two of us had built a quiet little world that felt complete.

But life has a way of expanding when you least expect it.

There were new faces ahead—ones who would become family. New dogs, each with their own quirks and stories, waiting to enter the picture. There would be laughter and chaos, muddy pawprints and chewed-up toys, long nights and even longer goodbyes. There would be lessons I didn't know I needed to learn—about patience, about letting go, about love in its purest, hardest form.

Looking back now, I realize that this chapter—the hikes, the rainy nights, the laughter echoing through that tiny camper— was our beginning. It was the time before life got louder, before the pack grew, before Clark's strength would be tested in ways neither of us could imagine.

In those quiet evenings with Clark's steady breathing beside me, I had no idea that I was living the prologue to something much bigger—a story of love, loyalty, and the kind of bond that doesn't end when the story does.

Clark was still just a puppy, full of energy and promise, standing at the start of a life that would intertwine completely with mine. And even though I couldn't see the whole path ahead, one thing was already clear: wherever life was going to take me, he'd be there velcroed to me through thick and thin.

Chapter Two: The Pack Begins

When Clark was around five months old, life had already settled into a comfortable rhythm. He'd grown out of his clumsy puppy stage and into the lanky, confident stride of a young Doberman. We had our patterns down—walks, hikes, long drives, hanging with my sister, evenings by the river. It was just the two of us, a team of sorts. Neither of us knew it yet, but everything was about to change.

That fall is when I met my wife. When I first brought Clark over to introduce him to his soon-to-be new family, he had no idea that his world was about to triple in size. At the time, she had two dogs of her own: Abbie, a muscular Pit-Lab mix with the kind of authority that filled a room, and Pete, a Beagle–Jack Russell blend with the soul of a grumpy old man.

Clark had already been learning the ways of the world from my sister's dog, Chyna. Chyna was all muscle and mischief— the kind of dog who didn't play gentle. She knocked Clark around just enough to teach him the ropes, to make him tougher, quicker, and smarter. By the time he met Abbie and Pete, he thought he had this "pack thing" figured out. He was wrong.

The first meeting was chaos in slow motion. Clark bounced into the yard, tail wagging, ears perked, ready to wrestle like he did with Chyna. Abbie wasn't impressed. Within seconds, she pinned him with one paw and gave him a low growl that translated perfectly: I'm in charge here. Pete, meanwhile, sat off to the side, squinting suspiciously at this tall, floppy-eared intruder. When Clark turned his charm toward him, Pete let out a sharp bark as if to say, Don't even think about it. From that moment on, their relationship was set: Pete would tolerate Clark's existence—but just barely.

Abbie, on the other hand, became a different kind of teacher. She was firm, commanding, and didn't play around. She immediately set the tone and let him know who was boss. During one rough play session, she nipped Clark hard enough to leave a few small cuts on his head. I was worried at first, but they healed quickly—and in their place, small patches of gray hair grew. Over time, a few more of those little gray spots appeared, each one like a battle medal earned under Abbie's watch. Those scars told their story: she was tough on him, but she was also shaping him.

In the early days, Clark tried to avoid Abbie altogether. It was comical watching him maneuver around her in the house, taking wide detours just to reach me without crossing her path. He literally would climb the edge of the couch on top of the backrest to get to us just to avoid her. But then came the day that changed everything.

We had left the dogs outside together while we went to work—something we'd done before without issue. When I came home, both of them were waiting by the gate, side by side, tails wagging like synchronized metronomes. It looked innocent enough—until I noticed the blood on Abbie's head.

She had a deep scrape, an avulsion on her scalp, probably from a quick scuffle that got out of hand. My medical instincts kicked in. I cleaned the wound, glued the skin back, and within minutes, she was patched up and acting like nothing happened. From that day on, something shifted between them. Whatever had happened in that yard wasn't just a fight—it was an understanding.

From then forward, Clark and Abbie were inseparable. They'd sit on the porch together, side by side, scanning the yard for squirrels or anything that didn't belong. They didn't need to play to connect—they just existed in perfect balance. Where she was the enforcer, he was the sentinel. Together, they ran that yard like a small kingdom.

Pete never quite joined their alliance. He remained the house curmudgeon, keeping his distance and muttering. But Clark respected him. He learned to read Pete's moods, to give him space, and occasionally to mimic his grumbling when something didn't go his way. It became one of his quirks—Clark's low, playful grumble when he was annoyed. It was pure Pete.

As months passed, our little pack found its rhythm. Clark grew stronger and more confident, but he also learned something deeper—restraint, patience, coexistence. Abbie and Pete had taught him that every pack needs balance, and not every battle is worth fighting.

When we got married and moved into a new home, it felt like a fresh start for everyone. The house had a fenced-in yard that felt like a dream come true—a safe haven for the dogs to roam freely. The neighborhood was full of kind people who adored animals. Neighbors would stop by the fence just to greet them, and everyone kept an eye out for one another. Clark loved standing at the gate, ears perked, tail wagging proudly, as if he'd personally taken on the role of neighborhood watch.

It was around that time that Mr. Kitty entered the picture.

My wife had rescued him from her workplace—one of a few stray kittens that had been hanging around the property. She caught one, had him neutered, and brought him home to recover for a few days. The plan was to release him once he healed. But like so many good intentions, that plan never stood a chance.

Mr. Kitty decided we were his people. And once he made that decision, there was no arguing.

He strutted around the house like he owned it, unbothered by the fact that three dogs were now watching him with curiosity. The first time Clark met him, he approached with caution. Mr. Kitty didn't flinch. Instead, he reached up and gave Clark a quick, deliberate smack on the nose. Clark froze, blinking in disbelief. Then, in true Clark fashion, he wagged his tail. Challenge accepted.

What followed was one of the most unexpected friendships I've ever seen. They played together constantly—Mr. Kitty swatting at Clark's face with lightning-fast paws, Clark dodging and weaving like a scene out of The Matrix. Sometimes, Clark would nudge Mr. Kitty gently with his nose, only to get another quick tap in return. It became their routine, their way of speaking.

Mr. Kitty wasn't intimidated by anyone, and in his own way, he became the alpha. The dogs respected him, even Abbie. He'd curl up on the porch railing while the three of them lounged below, keeping his watchful eye on the property. He wasn't just part of the pack—he was its overseer.

Every Christmas, the whole family—humans and dogs—took pictures with Santa. It became a tradition, something that perfectly captured the spirit of our little crew. Clark always looked regal in his holiday outfit, Abbie stoic, and Pete slightly annoyed. Those photos, year after year, told the story of a blended pack that worked because it was built on love, tolerance, and a little bit of chaos.

Clark grew up in that family. My stepson Nicolas, around thirteen at the time, adored him. They bonded instantly. Every evening, Clark would crawl into Nicolas's bed, curl up beside him, and stay there until morning. He waited by the window when the kids got off the school bus, wagging that nub tail, barking in excitement as if they'd been gone for weeks.

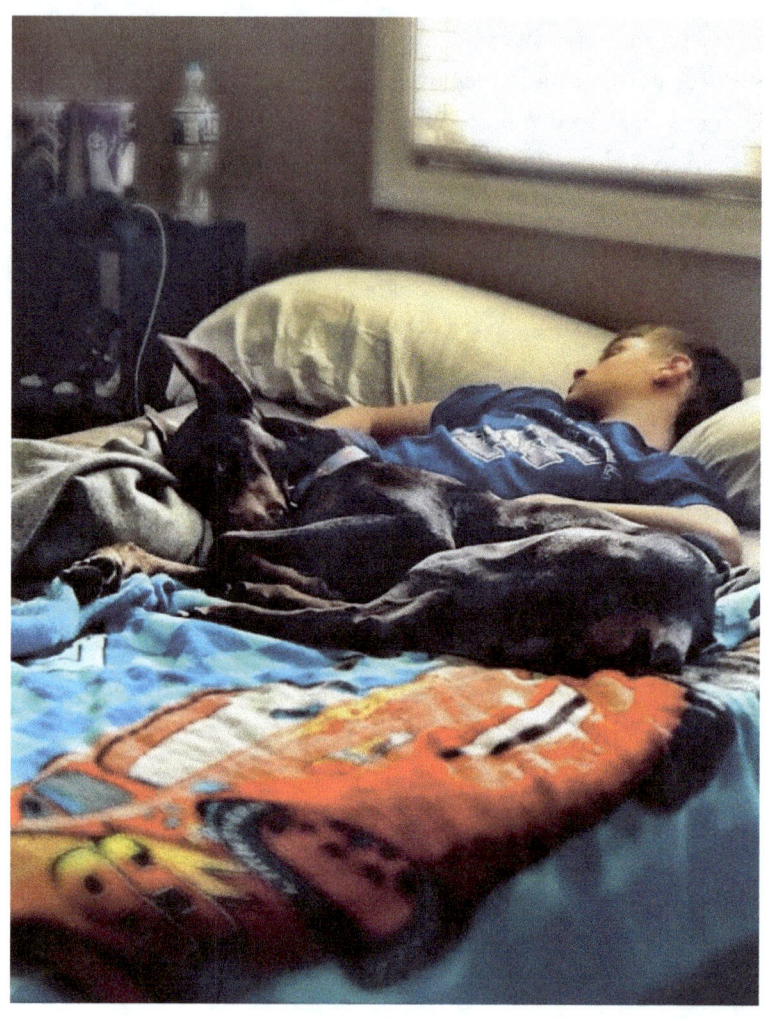

The kids filled their phones with pictures and videos of him—Snapchats, Instagram posts, endless memories of the dog who had once been mine alone but was now ours.

Our pack had grown, not just in number but in meaning. Clark had found his place. Watching him navigate this new chapter—with patience, humor, and loyalty—was like watching a reflection of my own growth. He had started as my dog, but he'd become the heartbeat of our family.

Reflection

Those were the golden years—the kind that slip by quietly until you look back and realize they were the best days of your life. The house was full, the yard was watched, and every evening ended with a dog at someone's feet. We didn't know it then, but we were storing up the ordinary miracles that would carry us through whatever came next. And as Clark settled into his place beside us—equal parts guardian, clown, and soul—our family's story began to write itself in pawprints.

Chapter Three: The Heart of the Family

By the time Clark reached a year and a half old, he had settled fully into family life. The clumsy puppy I once carried through the rain had grown into a strong, confident, and striking Doberman. His red rust coat gleamed in the sun, and his chest seemed to have broadened overnight. The bond we'd built through the long, quiet months in the camper had deepened into something much greater—he wasn't just my dog anymore. He was part of our family.

Every day, Clark was waiting at the door when I came home from work. He didn't just greet me; he embraced me. The moment I stepped through the door, I would kneel down and he'd rise up on his hind legs paws on my shoulders like he was giving a hug. It was his ritual—his way of saying, you're home now; everything's right again.

During the summers, he and Nicolas were inseparable. Nicolas would head outside the moment the sun was up, and Clark would follow close behind, tail whipping, eyes bright with excitement. They'd spend hours in the yard together—running, wrestling, exploring. In the winter, when the snow piled up, Clark discovered a new kind of joy. We'd make snowballs and toss them across the yard; he'd charge after them, catch them mid-air, and crush them with a triumphant shake. His bark would echo through the cold air, pure delight in every sound.

Across from the house was a two- or three-acre field—wide, open, and perfect for Clark's favorite game: frisbee. From the first throw, he was hooked. Training him was never about food—Clark wasn't food-motivated. He was driven by purpose, play, and praise. If there was a ball or frisbee involved, he'd give you everything he had.

We tried every kind of frisbee you could buy. The hard plastic ones cracked, the fabric ones tore, and the cheap ones never stood a chance. But then we found it—the Kong Flyer. Soft, flexible rubber, durable enough to withstand Clark's bite but light enough to soar. It became his frisbee, the one that could keep up with his energy. I'd hurl it across the field, and he'd take off like a rocket—legs stretched, body a blur, ears pinned back. He'd leap into the air, catch it mid-flight, and sprint straight back, laying it gently at my feet.

Clark wasn't a tug-of-war dog. He didn't see the point. He just wanted to play, to keep the game alive. He'd drop the frisbee right at my toes and stare up at me with that unmistakable again look. We could do that for hours, and often did. Those were the moments that made everything else fade away—the kind of pure, simple happiness that anchors itself in your memory forever.

Lessons in Discipline

As gentle as Clark was, there was one thing we had to work on: his pulling. Walking him on a leash in those early days was like trying to control a freight train made of enthusiasm. He was strong, curious, and headstrong—traits that made him incredible, but also challenging.

Eventually, I made the decision to send him to a two-week training program. It was hard being apart from him, but I knew he needed structure. When he came home, I could tell it had been good for him. He had matured. The trainer used a prong collar during his lessons—a tool that's often misunderstood.

A note about prong collars:

When used properly, a prong collar isn't a punishment—it's a communication tool. It distributes gentle, even pressure around the dog's neck, much like the way a mother dog corrects her pup with her mouth. The key is fit and technique: it should sit high on the neck, snug but not tight, and only be used with calm, corrective pressure, never force. The danger comes from misuse—jerking, over-tightening, or relying on it instead of positive reinforcement.

For Clark, it worked as intended: a reminder, not a restraint. I rarely had to touch it. Simply wearing it shifted his mindset— like a bridle on a horse. It told him, it's time to work.

After that, walking him was effortless. I'd say heel, and he'd slide right into position, matching my stride perfectly. When he was on the leash, he was all focus—eyes forward, body poised, alert but calm. He treated it like a job, and he took pride in doing it right.

I quickly learned that walking a Doberman in public draws attention. People would cross the street, pull their kids closer, or call out warnings like, "Better hold on to that one!" I always smiled politely, but it hurt a little every time. They didn't see the soft heart behind those alert ears—the dog who slept curled beside a thirteen-year-old boy, who cried when someone left the house, who wouldn't hurt a soul.

Dobermans get a bad reputation from misunderstanding. They play rough, they sound intense, and they look intimidating—but that's not aggression. That's energy, intelligence, and loyalty bundled together. Clark was proof that a powerful breed can also be the gentlest soul you'll ever meet. I learned to see those wary glances not as insults, but as opportunities—to show people that love and discipline could coexist beautifully.

Adventures & Rituals

Clark went everywhere we went. He was the definition of family dog. When Nicolas started racing motocross, Clark became the unofficial team mascot. On race weekends, he'd ride with us to the tracks, nose pressed to the window, ears twitching at every sound. We even shaved Nicolas's racing number—23—into Clark's fur on his back leg.

The other kids at the track adored him. He soaked up the attention, letting everyone pet him, pose for photos, and share snacks he wasn't supposed to have. He'd sit proudly by the bikes as if he was guarding them, his chest puffed and eyes steady.

At home, his days were full of small joys—porch naps, patrols along the fence, and barking at anything that dared to intrude on his kingdom. The lawnmower, the weed eater, and even the garbage truck were mortal enemies in Clark's mind. He took his duties seriously, and I often laughed watching him "protect" us from the neighbors mowing their yard.

He loved car rides more than anything. The moment I grabbed my keys, his ears would perk up. He always had to sit behind me, head poking between the seats, eyes locked on the road ahead. He'd rest his chin on my shoulder like a co-pilot, occasionally letting out a soft huff of contentment.

We took him hiking, exploring, and to the lake whenever we could. He loved the water—but couldn't swim to save his life. Literally. He'd wade in chest-deep, splashing with his front paws like a child, determined but hopeless. If you threw a stick too far, he'd paddle toward it in a panic, legs flailing, until I'd have to wade in and help him back. After that, he wore a lifejacket. Watching him paddle with it on—front legs flapping, eyes wide with determination—was comedy gold.

A Protector's Heart

As the years passed, Clark became deeply attuned to every emotion in our home. If someone was upset, he knew before a single word was spoken. He'd rest his head in your lap, look up with those amber eyes, and just be there.

When my wife was upset or stressed, Clark would shadow her closely, as if guarding her from her own worries. When my stepdaughter left for college, he moped for days—lying in her room, whining softly, waiting for her to return. And when she finally did, he'd cry out, grumble, and hugged her relentlessly, as if scolding her for being gone so long.

He was protective, but never possessive. When the kids' friends came over, he was gentle and watchful—always close enough to intervene, but never in the way. If one of the girls had a boyfriend visiting, Clark made sure he was present—quietly judging from the sidelines, tail still, eyes fixed, the silent guardian of the family.

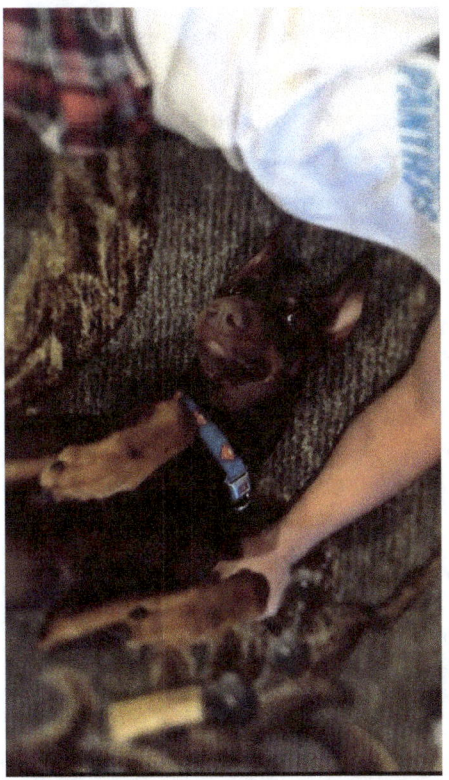

And then there were the lighter moments—the trampoline in the backyard, for example. Clark loved it. He'd jump up with the kids, bounce clumsily, then bark in delight as they laughed. He wasn't graceful, but he didn't care. Joy was joy, and he wanted to be part of it all.

He had become the heart of our home—the thread connecting everyone.

Reflection

Looking back on those years—ages one and a half through six—it's hard not to smile. They were simple, golden, and full of life. The kind of years you never realize you're living until they're gone. Clark wasn't just growing up; he was teaching us what it meant to love fully, to be present, and to find joy in the everyday.

He wasn't just part of our family.

He was the family.

And though we didn't know it at the time, those days—the frisbee throws in the field, the motocross weekends, the snowball games in the yard—would become the memories we'd hold onto the tightest.

Not because they led to something tragic or stormy—but because they were, in their quiet perfection, everything we didn't know we'd someday miss.

Chapter Four: The Rift in the Pack

By the time Clark turned six, our household had found its rhythm. The chaos of early years had softened into something steady, predictable, and full of life. Abbie, now older and gentler, spent most of her days lounging on the porch or pillow, content just to watch the world go by. Clark still nudged her into play every now and then, and though she'd humor him with a few zoomies while still letting him know whose boss, her body wasn't what it used to be. Pete, on the other hand, had grown grumpier with age — his eyes clouded a little, his patience thinner, his bark a bit sharper.

Around that time, two new members quietly joined the family. My stepdaughter rescued a kitten she named Pepper, a small ball of brown fur and green eyes, playful and mischievous from the start. Not long after, we took in another stray named Fred — a black cat with a calm, curious nature. Unlike the dogs, the cats slipped into the pack without much resistance. Fred especially had a gift for staying out of trouble, observing everything from a distance with an unshakable sense of ease. Pepper and Fred became fast friends, darting through the house in playful chases that ended in a pile of fur and purring on the couch. Even Clark, ever the gentle giant, learned to tolerate their antics.

Our home was full again — laughter, fur, chaos, and the warmth that only comes from shared love. But as with most families, time was slowly changing the balance.

A Lesson in the Holler

One weekend, while visiting my mom's place up in the holler of rural West Virginia, Clark learned a hard but necessary lesson. My mom's property had its share of stray dogs that came and went, each with their own place in an unspoken hierarchy. When Clark bounded into that world, frisbee in mouth, the other dogs took notice. One of the lower-ranked males decided to test him — lunging, snarling, trying to take the toy right from his mouth.

It was the first time I ever saw Clark truly defend himself. There was no hesitation, no panic — just instinct. A scuffle broke out, fast and loud, but it ended as quickly as it started. Clark stood tall afterward, breathing hard, chest out. There was no blood, just a lesson learned: sometimes, even good dogs have to stand their ground.

I didn't realize it then, but that moment would echo later in ways I never expected.

Cracks in the Pack

As the months went on, the relationship between Clark and Pete began to strain. They'd never been close, but age had made Pete more irritable. His joints were stiff, his eyes weaker, and his tolerance low. Clark, in his prime, still carried all that youthful energy. Sometimes, that alone was enough to set Pete off.

The first real incident was minor — just noise, a scuffle, and a yelp. Pete came away without injuries, but it was enough to remind us that tension was growing. We kept a closer eye on them after that.

We started using the outdoor kennel under the porch whenever we left the house. It gave the dogs space to be outside without direct supervision, and until then, it had worked perfectly. But one day, after being gone just a few hours, we returned home to find Pete bleeding. Our neighbor said they'd heard a commotion — growling, snapping, the kind of sound that makes your heart sink. We rushed Pete to the vet. He'd suffered a cut on his lip that needed repair, but he'd be okay. Still, something in Clark's eyes afterward looked different — not guilt, not fear, just confusion.

From that point on, we began separating them more intentionally. It worked for a while, though the air in the house always felt a little more cautious, a little more aware.

Then came the day that changed everything.

Bridge Day: A Celebration in the Gorge

Every October, the New River Gorge Bridge — the iconic
steel arch that crowns the heart of Fayetteville, West Virginia
— shuts down for one extraordinary day. Bridge Day is part
festival, part celebration, and part daredevil showcase. BASE
jumpers from all over the world come to leap from the 876-
foot span into the river below, parachutes billowing against
the autumn sky. For locals, it's more than just a spectacle; it's
a tradition, a gathering that draws tens of thousands to the
Gorge.

The day before the main event, a smaller celebration called
Taste of Bridge Day takes place at one of the local rafting
company grounds. It's a mix of live music, food vendors, and
community pride — a night where neighbors laugh, share
stories, and remind themselves what's special about living in
the New River region. Tourism from Bridge Day brings a
huge boost to the area's economy each year, spotlighting
small businesses, artisans, and the natural beauty that defines
our corner of Appalachia.

That evening, my wife and I attended the event. It was one of
those perfect autumn nights — crisp air, golden leaves, the
sound of laughter carrying across the field. We came home
tired but happy, ready to settle in and prepare for the next
day's festivities.

The Moment That Changed Everything

As soon as we got home, we let the dogs out for their usual evening routine. Clark went out first, stretching his legs, pacing the yard, and then came back in to eat. We always fed the dogs separately — Clark alone inside, while Abbie and Pete ate outside. It had become second nature.

I was in the kitchen filling the coffee pot for the morning, the sound of water running steady and calm. Clark was eating, moving back and forth between his bowl and the counter where I stood. He was always that way — never just eating, always checking in, circling the room as if making sure everyone was okay.

Then, in a flash, everything changed.

Pete slipped between Clark and his food bowl unnoticed. I heard the low growl from Pete before I even turned my head. It wasn't long or loud — just the sound of two dogs who'd reached a breaking point. I looked over, and before I could move, Pete lunged.

Clark reacted on instinct. It happened faster than thought — a blur of motion, a sound I'll never forget. My wife and I dropped everything and ran. Pete was caught in Clark's mouth, both of them struggling, fear and pain in the air. I grabbed Clark by the collar and pried his jaws open, freeing

Pete from his grip. Both dogs were trembling, terrified, Pete bleeding.

My wife rushed in and immediately pulled Clark away, closing him off in another room while I knelt beside Pete. Blood ran from his neck — deep, dark, and fast. I pressed my hands against the wound, talking to him, coaching him to hang on. Within a few minutes, we were in the car, racing toward the nearest vet twenty minutes away. It felt like hours.

But despite everything — the pressure, the prayers, the speed — Pete didn't make it. He was gone before we arrived.

Aftermath

The days that followed were heavy. My wife was devastated — Pete had been with her long before I came into the picture. He was her little shadow, her constant. The house felt strange without him, as if his small presence had filled more space than we realized.

There was anger, confusion, and guilt. For her, for me, even for Clark. I understood her pain, but I also knew — deep down — that Clark hadn't done it out of malice. He'd reacted out of fear, or defense, or pure instinct. It didn't make it easier, but it made it real.

We separated him for a while, unsure of what to do. I watched him closely, looking for signs of aggression, fear, anything that might suggest this was more than an accident. But there was nothing. Clark went back to being Clark — gentle, loyal, loving. He never so much as raised a lip to another animal again.

That's the hardest part about moments like that — the way they live in two truths. The first is grief: the weight of loss, the haunting what-ifs. The second is understanding: that nature isn't cruel, just indifferent, and sometimes even love can't stop instinct.

Reflection

That night changed our family. It took time — time to forgive, time to heal, time to see Clark again for who he was, not what had happened.

I carried guilt for not seeing it coming, for not doing more to prevent it. But I also carried grace — for both dogs. Pete had been tired, old, and proud. Clark had been strong, young, and loyal. Somewhere between those two truths, tragedy found its space.

In the years that followed, Clark remained the same sweet soul he'd always been. He played with Abbie, curled beside us on the couch, and greeted me every night at the door with that same eager hug. But for me, something deeper had shifted. I understood him now in a way I hadn't before — his instincts, his loyalty, his fragility.

Looking back, I don't think of that night as "the storm." It wasn't a storm. It was a fracture — one that hurt deeply, but also reminded me that life, even in its most painful moments, is still threaded with love and forgiveness.

Clark didn't lose our trust. He didn't lose his place. If anything, we loved him harder after that. Because sometimes the hardest part of loving deeply is learning to accept that even in perfection, life finds its cracks.

And somehow, we still keep going.

Chapter Five: Second Chances

By the time Clark was about seven and a half years old, our lives had settled into a rhythm that felt easy again. The weight of losing Pete had faded into something quieter—still tender, but no longer sharp. Clark had healed in his own way too. He was happy, content, and back to being the guardian of the household—steady, affectionate, and always ready with his trademark hug when I walked through the door at the end of the day.

We thought we'd found our balance. But as it so often happens, life had another plan.

A Call from Kansas

It started with a phone call that my wife received one afternoon.

She's the kind of person everyone calls when there's an animal in need—deeply connected with local rescues, the Humane Society, and a network of animal lovers across the region. This time, it was a friend of hers who knew a man struggling with a young Doberman he'd bought from a breeder in Kansas.

The man, who worked long hours and traveled constantly, simply couldn't give the dog the care she needed. He planned to drive her all the way back to the breeder—Douglas—

because he didn't want her to end up in the wrong hands. But until then, he needed someone to look after her.

"Would you two be willing to babysit her for a little while?" my wife asked.

She barely finished the sentence before I said yes. I think she already knew the answer to this question since she knew my love for this particular breed of dog.

When the man arrived a few days later, he parked out front and waved me over. The sight caught me off guard: in the backseat sat a small, nervous black and tan female Doberman, about fourteen weeks old. Her eyes were wide and uncertain, and she didn't make a sound.

The man opened the door and gently reached for her, but she wouldn't budge. He finally had to pick her up and set her on the ground beside the car. The moment her paws hit the driveway, she crouched low, trembling, and had a little nervous pee. The smell of stale confinement clung to her coat—she must have been left too long in her crate, forced to use the bathroom where she slept.

It broke my heart.

She looked fragile and unsure, her ears half-folded back, every movement cautious. I crouched beside her, spoke softly, and after a moment she inched closer, nose twitching, eyes searching mine. Something passed between us right then—a silent understanding. She didn't know it yet, but she was home.

First Impressions

I led her to the backyard so she could stretch her legs and start exploring. For a while, she stayed glued to me, sniffing cautiously, glancing over her shoulder as if afraid the man might come back to take her away. Then she started to sniff out the other animal's scents everywhere she walked to gain familiarity. Once she settled in, the running began.

Then it was time for the real introduction.

Clark.

He trotted out from the porch, chest out, tail wagging with curiosity. The moment he saw her, he froze. His head tilted, ears perked, and his entire posture changed—alert, but excited. I held her leash tightly as the two met nose to nose. She trembled, but Clark's tail began whipping faster and faster until his whole back end wiggled.

He circled her twice, then suddenly darted sideways, letting out a playful bark that said everything words couldn't: let's play. It was as if she was the most beautiful thing he had ever seen.

At first, she didn't know what to do. She just stood there, unsure. But when he barked again—lower, softer, inviting—she took off after him. Within seconds they were racing across the yard, kicking up dirt and leaves, the older Doberman showing the little one what it meant to run free.

It was chaos. It was clumsy. It was perfect.

Finding Their Rhythm

The first few days were a mix of excitement and uncertainty. Clark went through all the stages of emotion you'd expect from a big brother who didn't ask for a sibling—thrilled at first, then annoyed, then distant, then finally accepting.

She wanted his attention every second of the day, shadowing his every move. If he laid down, she laid down. If he drank water, she had to drink too. If he grabbed a toy, she grabbed the same one. She tried to steal his sticks every chance she had. Clark, ever the gentleman, tolerated it with heroic patience, though his eyes sometimes said, you've got to be kidding me. His voice in that low grumble that he had learned from Pete.

Abbie, on the other hand, wasn't impressed. The old matriarch didn't care who this little whirlwind was—she made sure everyone knew she was still the boss. One firm growl and Xena (as she'd soon be called) learned quickly to keep a respectful distance.

Inside, Fred and Mr. Kitty watched the new arrival with measured disinterest. They'd seen this kind of chaos before. Fred, the observer, preferred to stay curled in a sunny spot by the window, while Mr. Kitty, self-appointed ruler of the house, flicked his tail and pretended none of it concerned him.

But despite all the shifting dynamics, something warm began to settle in.

Becoming Xena

After a few days, my wife and I started calling her Xena—after the warrior princess. The name fit perfectly.

At first, we truly believed she was only staying with us temporarily until her owner got his life in order. However, each time we tried to reach him, communication became increasingly difficult. Calls went unanswered, texts unread. Weeks passed, and it became clear he wasn't coming back for her.

That's when we reached out directly to Douglas, the breeder in Kansas. He listened patiently as we explained everything—her condition, her progress, the bond she'd formed with us and Clark. His voice softened. "If she's found her place with you," he said, "then she's right where she belongs."

A few signatures later, Xena was officially ours.

Clark, meanwhile, seemed both bewildered and resigned. He grumbled occasionally when she climbed over him or stole his favorite toy, but there was affection behind it. She'd curl up beside him after their rough-and-tumble play, her small body tucked against his chest, and he'd rest his chin on her head with a sigh that seemed to say, fine—you can stay.

The house was alive again, full of movement, sound, and love.

The Surgery

Of course, there was one major problem left—Clark was still intact, and Xena was a young, healthy female. We didn't want to take any chances. Scheduling his neuter surgery felt necessary but strangely emotional. He'd always been my strong, confident boy, and part of me worried how he'd handle it.

That morning, as we pulled into the vet's office, he pressed his nose against the window, watching the world roll by with his usual calm. He walked inside without hesitation, tail swishing, unaware of what was ahead. When we picked him up later, though, the look he gave me said everything. His eyes drooped with betrayal, the infamous cone of shame amplifying his heartbreak. If a dog could pout, Clark had mastered it.

The following days were tough. He developed a large hematoma where his scrotum had been, and it swelled painfully. We had to restrict his movement, apply cold compresses, and make several follow-up visits to ensure there were no complications. Through it all, he whined and fussed and milked the sympathy for everything it was worth.

But the sweetest part was watching Xena—the same little ball of chaos who'd been terrorizing him for weeks—change her behavior completely. She'd lie beside him, quiet and still, as if she knew he needed her calm. She watched over him in silence, only moving when he did. And for the first time, I saw Clark truly accept her—not as a guest, not as a rival, but as family.

A Gentle Change

Once he'd healed, something in Clark was different. He was calmer, more thoughtful, a little slower to react. It wasn't age exactly—it was more like perspective. The youthful energy that once defined him had settled into a grounded, peaceful presence.

He and Xena began to move together like two halves of the same soul—different energies, but perfectly balanced. When they played, the house sounded like a war zone—paws thundering, growls echoing—but it was pure joy.

Abbie watched them with patient disapproval from her spot on the couch, occasionally grumbling when they got too close. Fred and Mr. Kitty supervised from their corners like referees, unimpressed but accepting.

And just like that, our home felt whole again.

A New Home Ahead

By the time the year began winding down, life felt good. So good, in fact, that my wife and I decided it was time for a new beginning of our own.

We'd found a beautiful house an hour away—a place with a wide yard, plenty of tall trees, and room for all of us to stretch out. The moment we stepped onto that property, we knew it was meant to be. We just had to ensure the property was dog-friendly.

Clark and Xena didn't know what was coming, but I think they sensed it. They watched as we packed boxes, followed us from room to room, curious about the sudden activity. Clark would sit quietly, head tilted, as Xena darted around with her usual mischief—grabbing tape rolls, stealing packing paper, turning every chore into a game.

It was chaos, but the kind that makes you smile.

As I stood there watching them—Clark steady and strong, Xena wild and full of life—I felt a deep sense of peace. After everything we'd been through, it felt like we were standing on the edge of something new, something good.

Reflection

When Xena came into our lives, it wasn't planned. We thought we were helping a stranger, doing a small kindness. But like so many of the best things in life, she turned out to be a gift we didn't know we needed. She helped heal the quiet spaces Pete had left behind. She reminded Clark what it meant to play, to teach, to love again. And she brought laughter back to our home in ways we couldn't have imagined.

Clark, my steadfast companion, had found his balance once more—not through solitude, but through connection. And as we prepared to move into our new home, I realized that what we'd built together wasn't just a pack. It was a family—one bound by loyalty, forgiveness, and the simple, unwavering truth that love always finds a way to fill the empty spaces.

Chapter Six: The New Home

January arrived with a cold stillness that felt like a clean slate. After years in our old house, filled with laughter, memories, and paw prints, we were finally ready for a fresh start. We closed on our new home on January 4th, and before the ink was even dry on the paperwork, I was already unloading boxes.

It wasn't just about the move—it was about building a space where our family, both human and four-legged, could grow into the next chapter together.

Settling the Land

With three dogs and two cats, priority number one was making sure everyone would be safe and comfortable. The new house sat on roughly four acres of rolling, tree-dotted land—a dream for us and a paradise for the dogs. Sticks galore!

But paradise needed boundaries.

Having two Dobermans now, I knew we couldn't rely on chance or cheap equipment. So I coordinated the installation of a high-quality invisible dog fence to begin the very day we closed. As the technician pulled up to start mapping the perimeter, Clark stood in the driveway beside me, head high, tail wagging, watching every movement like he was personally supervising the project.

As my trusty companion, he was tasked with ensuring that the house was ready for the other animals. We knew that some of the neighbors may be fearful of two Dobermans. That is why we needed to be one hundred percent sure that we had the best underground fence installed.

By that evening, the fence was live. It was then Clark tested and approved.

He'd been trained on invisible fences before, and within minutes he figured out the new property's limits—stopping precisely at the invisible line, tilting his head in thought, and turning back toward the house as if to say, got it. His intelligence always amazed me. He didn't need much teaching; he just seemed to understand.

The yard, thick with trees and scattered branches, became his playground. It was winter still, the ground cold and littered with fallen sticks, but to Clark, that was heaven. He spent hours dragging them around, breaking them into pieces, and proudly dropping them at my feet for another throw.

He was in his element—joyful, strong, free.

Leaving the Old Behind

The move stretched over a month. Every trip between houses felt bittersweet.

That old home had seen so much of our life—the early days of Clark's puppyhood, his friendship with Abbie and Pete, the laughter of the kids playing in the yard, the frisbee games at sunset. Standing in that backyard for the last time, I couldn't help but feel the weight of every memory pressing against the cold winter air.

There were tears, but also excitement. A new home meant new space, new beginnings. It felt like the next step in a story we'd been writing together for years.

By the end of the month, we were officially settled. The boxes were mostly unpacked, the animals had claimed their favorite spots, and life began to take shape again.

A Kingdom to Watch Over

Clark and Xena adapted quickly to the new place. They explored every inch of the yard, running side by side like a matched set of sentinels—two Dobermans, black and rust against the pale winter grass, scanning for anything that didn't belong.

The front porch became their post. They'd sit side by side at the top of the steps, ears erect, eyes sharp, watching the world like twin statues guarding a fortress. If a stranger so much as walked near the road, they'd dart toward the invisible fence line, stopping precisely at the boundary, barking just enough to say, we see you.

Of course, anyone who actually knew them could have easily defused the whole thing by tossing a tennis ball. Their fierce stares melted the moment play entered the equation. Beneath all that muscle and posture, they were just two pushovers with big hearts.

Inside, Fred and Mr. Kitty resumed their reign. Fred continued his quiet watch from the window ledge, while Mr. Kitty made it clear that the new house was his domain, too.

By the time spring rolled around, everyone had found their rhythm again. The house was alive with sound and energy— the tapping of claws on hardwood, the jingling of collars, the hum of ordinary happiness.

The Summer Weekend

By mid-summer, the house felt completely like home. The yard was cleared, the invisible fence had proven itself reliable, and we were spending most weekends outside.

One weekend, we had a friend named Teresa come stay with us. Clark, who never met a stranger, fell head over heels for her. He followed her from room to room, leaned against her leg like he'd known her forever, and even insisted on sleeping beside her upstairs. She didn't mind—she adored him.

That Saturday, we were all outside enjoying the sun. Teresa and I were taking turns throwing sticks for Clark while Xena bounded around chasing leaves trying to take the sticks we were throwing to Clark. Clark was full of life—charging through the grass, nubby tail high, eyes bright. Everything about the day felt easy, like the world was exactly as it should be.

Later that evening, after dinner and laughter, things quieted down. Clark was under my wife's desk, his usual safe spot—a habit from the old days at my sister's house while she worked. I saw him in there and coaxed him into coming into the living room. He followed me and curled up on the couch.

I went to sit beside him, leaned down to hug him like I always did—and he yelped.

A sharp, sudden cry.

It startled both of us. Clark never cried out like that. Always tough, he looked at me with confused eyes, breathing shallowly. I backed off immediately, giving him space, assuming maybe I'd just leaned on him wrong. He seemed to settle after that, so we let him rest for the night.

The First Signs

The next morning, something wasn't right.

When I let Clark out, I noticed a faint weakness in his hind legs, in particularly the left. At first, I brushed it off— Dobermans are known for sliding a bit on hardwood floors, especially as they get older. But as he stepped down the porch stairs, I saw it clearly: his balance was off. His back end swayed slightly, his movements unsure. His gait was definitely off.

He hesitated at the last step, something he'd never done before. Then, when he finally reached the grass, he moved stiffly—slow, cautious, careful.

I followed him, trying to figure out what was wrong. I checked his paws, pressed gently along his spine, testing for pain. Nothing. Then I reached under his neck to lift his head slightly—and he cried out again.

It was a short, sharp yelp, filled with pain and fear. My heart sank. Something was wrong. Deeply wrong.

I knew right then that as soon as I got home that evening, we'd be going straight to the vet.

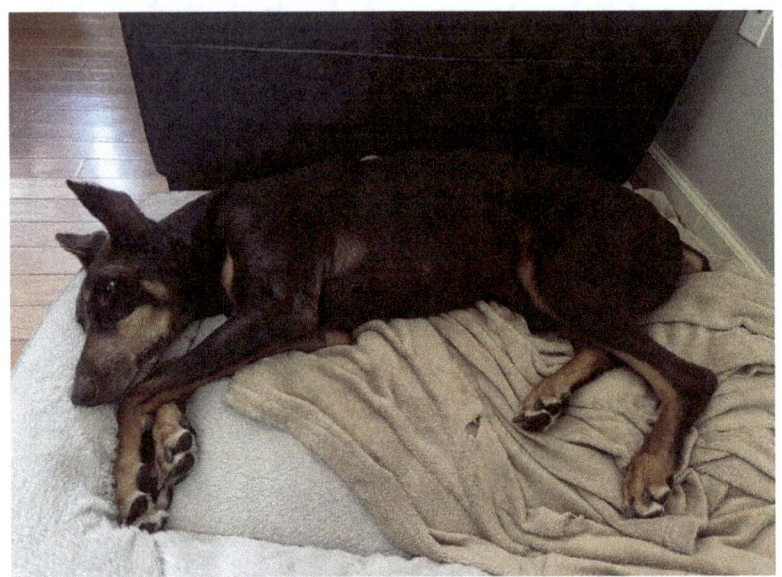

That morning was the first time I saw the shadow of what was coming—the beginning of Clark's fight with what we would soon learn was a spinal condition. At that moment, I didn't know the name for it. I didn't know the road we were about to walk together.

All I knew was that something inside the strongest dog I'd ever known had shifted.

And that I would do whatever it took to help him.

Chapter Seven: The Fighter Within

The night Clark cried out in pain, my stomach dropped. It was sharp, sudden, and unlike anything I'd ever heard from him. He'd been fine moments before—resting on the couch, calm and content—but that sound cut through the house like a warning bell. I knew instantly that something wasn't right.

We gave him space that evening, hoping it was just a strained muscle or an awkward twist. But by morning, it was clear this was something deeper. When I let him out, his back end wobbled slightly. His left hind leg dragged just enough to make my heart race. He walked slowly, carefully, as if his body had betrayed his confidence overnight.

When I lifted his head to check his neck, he yelped again. That was all I needed to know.

I spent the rest of the day at work sick with worry, counting down the hours until I could rush home. By the time I got there, Clark was struggling to stand. He'd try to rise, only to lean or fall to the side, mostly on that weak back leg. Something neurological—my mind went there immediately.

We went straight to the vet. They examined him gently, testing his reflexes and watching his stance. It confirmed what I already suspected—there was a deficit, likely spinal or nerve-related. The vet prescribed prednisone, a steroid to reduce inflammation, and told us to restrict his movement. We started the medication as soon as we got home.

By the next day, I saw a glimmer of the old Clark returning. He still stumbled, but there was more strength in his steps, more focus in his eyes. The medicine seemed to help. He was improving, though the hardest part was keeping him calm. Xena wanted to play, as always, and Clark—ever the pleaser—didn't want to say no. We had to separate them often, especially around the stairs.

Within three days, new challenges appeared. Clark began leaking urine, small puddles on the floor. It was clear the prednisone was affecting him. We put him in a soft diaper and did our best to make him comfortable, all while counting the days until his follow-up visit.

When we returned to the vet, his mobility had improved, but not completely. There was still a slight drop-foot in his left hind leg. I asked about every possible cause, including Lyme disease—because we lived in the woods, in a region thick with deer ticks, and Clark had spent years exploring every inch of it.

Even though he'd been vaccinated, Lyme disease can occasionally slip past immunity. It's caused by Borrelia burgdorferi, a bacteria transmitted by ticks after they've been attached for 24 hours or more. In dogs, it can cause lameness that shifts from one leg to another, joint swelling, fever, fatigue, and in severe cases, kidney or heart involvement. Some dogs show no signs at all until the disease is advanced. Living where we did—nearly inside a national forest—Lyme was always a concern.

But the symptoms didn't quite line up perfectly. That's when my mind turned to something even more specific to Dobermans.

Clark, being a purebred, carried with him all the strengths—and vulnerabilities—of his breed. Dobermans are known for their intelligence, loyalty, and athleticism, but they're also prone to several genetic conditions. One is Dilated Cardiomyopathy (DCM), a heart disease that causes the heart muscle to thin and weaken until it can no longer pump effectively. In Dobermans, it's heartbreakingly common—often silent until it's too late. Two genetic mutations, called DCM 1 and DCM 2, are responsible for most cases.

Then there's Cervical Spondylomyelopathy, better known as Wobbler Syndrome. It's a spinal condition where the vertebrae in the neck compress the spinal cord, causing pain, weakness, or loss of coordination in the hind legs. Many Dobermans begin showing signs between ages six and eight—exactly where Clark was now.

The more I read, the more the pieces started to make sense. His wobbling, his reluctance to lift his head, the intermittent pain—it all pointed toward a spinal issue. Still, I wanted to rule out everything else. So the vet ran tests for Lyme and prescribed antibiotics, just in case.

Over the next several weeks, we gradually weaned him off the prednisone. The incontinence stopped, and his energy began to return. He wasn't 100%, but he was better—steady enough to walk, play, and even run again, though with a faint limp that never fully went away.

He adjusted beautifully. It was as if Clark knew his limits now. He wouldn't leap in the air like he normally would. He'd still chase sticks and sprint through the yard, but when he'd had enough, he'd simply stop, lie down, and watch the world. He stood in his own way that something inside him had changed, but instead of fighting it, he learned to adapt.

Loss and Resilience

That same year brought another kind of heartbreak.

In August, we lost Mr. Kitty. He had been with us since the early days—a watchful presence who ruled the house with quiet authority. His absence left a strange silence behind. Clark and Xena both felt it. They'd often lie near his favorite chair, as if waiting for him to return.

Clark had always shared a special bond with him. It wasn't unusual to find the two of them lying back-to-back on the living room rug, content just to share space. Mr. Kitty had been his companion, his shadow. Losing him hurt all of us, but I could see it most in Clark's eyes—the way he'd glance at the window ledge where Mr. Kitty used to sit, then look at me, as if asking where he'd gone.

Life, though, has a way of moving forward.

Back to the Good Days

Through the fall and into winter, Clark adjusted to his "new normal." He still had a slight weakness in his left leg, but he never let it slow him down. We didn't restrict him much anymore—he seemed to know when to take it easy.

By spring, he was back outside, helping with yard work like he always did. When I chopped wood or cleared brush, Clark and Xena turned it into a game. They'd collect sticks, drag them across the yard, and occasionally steal entire piles I'd just finished stacking. Watching them together made everything feel right again.

That summer, we bought a pontoon boat. Every weekend, we'd load up and drive to the lake, about twenty-five minutes away. Clark wasn't a natural swimmer, but he loved the water. One weekend, we decided to bring all the dogs. We beached the boat on a small island and threw sticks into the shallows.

Clark, determined as ever, launched himself into the lake after every throw. He couldn't swim well—his front legs churned the water more than moved it—but he never gave up. When he tired out, I'd wade in and help guide him back to shore, where he'd shake off, proud and dripping, ready to try again.

Xena wasn't much better at swimming, though she gave it her best effort. Maybe it was a Doberman thing.

Those were good days.

The Subtle Shift

By late August, life felt stable again. The dogs were healthy, the house was full, and everything seemed calm.

Then one evening, after a long day of yard work, I let Clark and Xena out as usual. When we called them back in, Clark went straight under my wife's desk—his safe spot. That was the first sign something wasn't right.

He trembled softly, his body tight with discomfort. I knew the look. It was the same look he'd had the first time this all started.

The next morning, his limp was worse. His back end seemed weaker again. The fear crept back in—the thought that maybe this wasn't just a flare-up, but a progression.

It was the weekend, and the vet wouldn't be open until Monday. We did what we could: kept him confined to his crate, gave him natural anti-inflammatories, and prayed we could keep him comfortable until help was available.

I sat beside his crate that night, my hand resting on his shoulder, feeling the warmth of his breathing.

He was still my Clark—still alert, still loving, still fighting.

But in that quiet moment, I could feel it: the battle we thought we'd won wasn't over.

Reflection

Those months tested more than Clark's body—they tested our hearts. Watching him fight his way back, wobbling but determined, reminded me what resilience really looks like. He didn't dwell on what he'd lost or what might come next. He just met each day with quiet courage, tail still wagging, eyes still bright with trust. It struck me how dogs don't fear the future the way we do—they simply live in the love they have right now. And in that season of uncertainty, Clark became my teacher once again. Every careful step he took was a reminder to keep moving, to keep believing, and to find peace in the fight itself. Even then, as I sat beside him listening to his steady breathing, I couldn't have known how much further that fight would go—or how deeply it would change us both.

Chapter Eight — The Road to Ohio

It always seems to happen on a weekend.

Friday night had been uneventful. Clark had gone outside, eaten, and curled up in his favorite spot near my wife's desk. But by Saturday morning, I knew something was off. He didn't come to greet me with his usual stretch and tail wag. Instead, he stayed still, eyes alert but body trembling — a quiet signal that something inside him had gone wrong again.

He could barely stand. When he tried to move, his back legs wobbled beneath him like they'd forgotten how to do their job. I helped him outside, but he refused to use the bathroom. Clark had always been a bit of a "particular" pooper — he needed the right spot, the right mood, the right sense of safety. But now he simply couldn't steady himself. His body wasn't obeying him anymore.

And of course, the vet was closed.

The Longest Weekend

That weekend stretched into eternity. My wife and I traded updates constantly. She worked from home and stayed close to him while I was at work, sending me texts every few hours.

"He's resting now."

"He tried to stand but sat right back down."

"He's drinking water but won't eat."

I stared at those messages between patients, heart pounding, waiting for Monday like it was a lifeline.

By Monday morning, Clark's decline was undeniable. He struggled to rise, and when he did, his back end dragged behind him. The look in his eyes wasn't just pain — it was confusion. I rushed home, loaded him carefully into the car, and headed straight for the vet.

The Return to the Vet

The moment we walked in, it felt like déjà vu. Same exam room. Same quiet sympathy in the vet's voice. We were discharged with prednisone and a muslce relaxer.

Prednisone had become a familiar double-edged sword. It's a corticosteroid, powerful in reducing inflammation around the spinal cord, but it comes with a list of side effects that can wear both a body and a household down — panting, hunger, restlessness, muscle loss, even urinary leakage. We'd seen all of that before. Still, we knew it could buy Clark time and comfort.

This time, the vet adjusted his meds — a stronger combination designed not only to reduce swelling but to ease nerve pain and muscle spasms. We left with a small paper bag full of hope and a receipt that didn't matter. Whatever it cost, it was worth it.

Within three days, Clark was showing small signs of improvement. He could stand with help, and he even managed to shuffle a few steps. We clung to that progress.

That weekend, we had a charity ride planned — an ATV benefit event we did every year to raise money for children with leukemia. It meant a lot to us, but the thought of leaving Clark behind, leaking urine and unable to move well, didn't sit right. So we brought him along.

We folded down the back seats of the Polaris RZR Turbo R4 and laid down thick bedding so he could ride in comfort. The trails that day were gentle — wide, rolling, and peaceful. Clark sat proudly between us, wind in his face, eyes half-closed like he was remembering younger days when his legs still worked the way they should. People stopped to pet him, to talk to him, to tell us how beautiful he was. For a few hours, it felt like things might be okay.

But by that night, his legs had failed him again.

Seeking Answers

Sunday was another endless day of waiting for Monday. When the clinic finally opened, we went back for what felt like the hundredth time. The vet looked over his chart, noting his previous episodes — the first when he was eight, now again at nine — and explained that this could be progression of an underlying neurological disorder.

We discussed every option on the table: more medication, advanced imaging, even surgery. None of it felt right. We weren't ready to give up, but we also weren't ready to put him through something without knowing everything we could.

That's when I brought up The Ohio State University College of Veterinary Medicine. I'd done my research. Their Veterinary Medical Center in Columbus is one of the leading facilities in the nation for canine neurology, particularly for large breeds like Dobermans. Their team includes board-certified specialists in neurosurgery, orthopedic surgery, and cardiology, and they're widely recognized for their work with Wobbler Syndrome and Dilated Cardiomyopathy (DCM) — two conditions that too often go hand-in-hand in Dobermans.

We were lucky to live within driving distance — about five hours. Some owners fly their dogs across the country to get to Ohio State. We didn't hesitate. We requested the referral immediately.

The Road North

The following week, my wife and I both took time off work. By then, Clark's back legs had weakened so much that I'd bought a sling to help him outside. I'd also ordered a dog wheelchair, preparing for whatever the future held. Even with his struggles, Clark still wagged his tail when we loaded him into the truck. His eyes said what words couldn't: I trust you.

The drive to Columbus was quiet. When we arrived, it didn't feel like a typical vet clinic. The facility was spotless, organized, calm — no smell of disinfectant, no barking chaos. Just quiet competence.

The staff treated Clark like he mattered, not just as a patient, but as a soul. After a thorough exam, the neurologist explained their concern: multifocal Wobbler's disease — meaning multiple sites of spinal cord compression, rather than a single spot.

When a dog has one compression site, surgery can often relieve pressure effectively. But in multifocal disease, the degeneration occurs across several vertebrae, making surgical success uncertain. In these cases, medical management — anti-inflammatories, nerve-pain control, and muscle relaxants — often becomes the safer path.

Still, before they could proceed with imaging or anesthesia, the doctors wanted a cardiology consultation. Dobermans are genetically predisposed to Dilated Cardiomyopathy (DCM) — a condition where the heart muscle thins and weakens, reducing its ability to pump efficiently. Two known gene mutations, DCM1 and DCM2, are often the culprits. Because anesthesia stresses the heart, it's standard protocol for Dobermans to undergo an echocardiogram before any procedure.

The cardiologist confirmed early-stage DCM — not yet severe, but present. His heart was still strong, and they started him on pimobendan, a medication that helps strengthen heart contractions and improve blood flow. It was preventive, but necessary.

After hours of discussion, weighing every risk and option, we chose not to pursue surgery. Clark's age, the multifocal nature of the disease, and the anesthesia risks made it clear that the best path forward was comfort and quality of life. The team adjusted his medications — high-dose prednisone to control inflammation, gabapentin for nerve pain, and amantadine to modulate pain pathways.

Each medication served its role:

•Prednisone reduced the swelling around his spinal cord, buying him relief at a cost to his energy and muscle mass.

•Gabapentin soothed the electric sting of nerve pain.

•Amantadine, often used in combination with other analgesics, worked to "reset" the brain's pain response.

We loaded up his new prescriptions, a few weeks' supply of hope', and began the drive home.

Two Steps Forward, Three Back

The next few weeks followed a cruel rhythm.

When his prednisone dose was high, Clark could walk again — stiffly, but proud. We'd lower the dose, as directed, and within a day or two, he'd stumble and weaken. Every Wednesday, the taper hit, and every Thursday, he'd decline. By Friday, he'd look at me with tired eyes, as if asking Why can't I just stay better?

By October, the pattern had worn us thin. His bad days outnumbered the good. He stopped showing interest in toys. He didn't want to play. He barely moved except to shift positions or to greet me softly when I came home. The prednisone had taken its toll — the panting, the muscle loss, the restlessness.

One Monday, he trembled all day, unable to find comfort. I sat with him that night, my hand resting on his side, whispering to him the same way I had when he was a puppy: We'll get through this, buddy. Just hold on.

By morning, he surprised me. He stood — weak, wobbly, but standing. It was a small miracle, and he gave us five good days after that. We cherished every one of them.

But the following weekend, he fell again. By Monday, he had lost all function of his back legs. Completely paralyzed.

Reflection

There's a kind of silence that settles in moments like that — not the kind that's peaceful, but the kind that feels like time itself holding its breath. Watching Clark lose what made him so alive broke something in me. He had always been motion — running, jumping, chasing, protecting, loving. Now, his world had shrunk to a bed, a sling, and the spaces between my hands.

But even then, he didn't give up. His eyes stayed bright. His spirit, somehow, stronger than ever.

In that stillness, I learned something about love I'll never forget — that real love is staying, even when staying hurts.

Chapter 9: The Hardest Promise

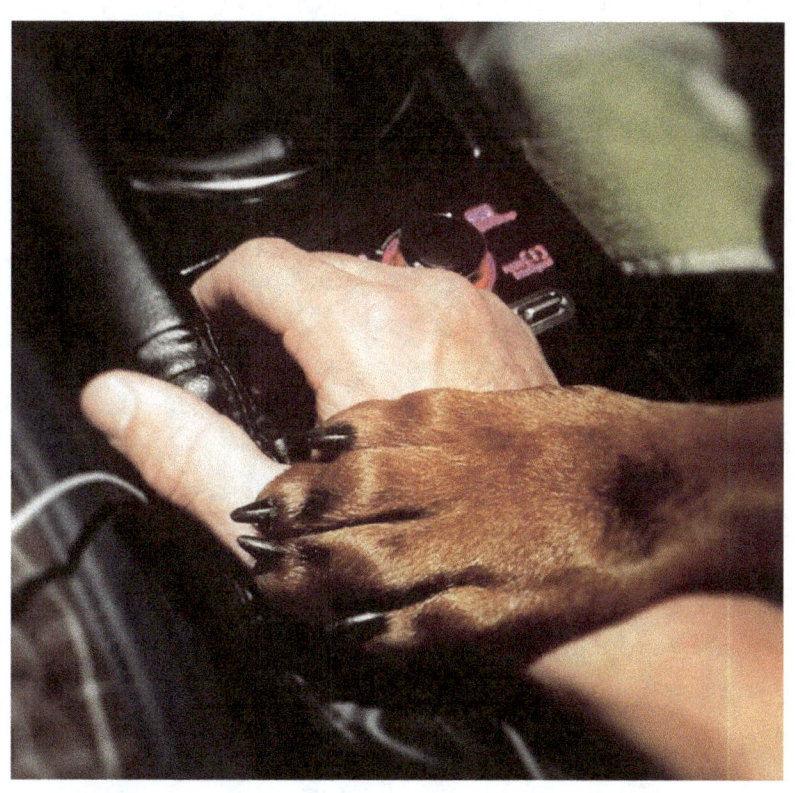

By October, Clark had been fighting for months. His spirit was still there — steady, loyal, and full of quiet courage — but his body was betraying him piece by piece. We'd gone through good days and bad ones, but even his "good" days were only shadows of what they once were. He no longer played with his toys or ran through the yard barking at the wind. His tail barely wagged. His head hung lower. His once-powerful stride had turned into an uneven shuffle — a careful balancing act on legs that no longer obeyed. Xena even knew something was wrong. She would only attempt to play when he was having one of his 'good' days.

When he did have a spark of his old self, it was like a glimpse through a window — the Clark I knew bursting through for a fleeting moment. He'd see a stick and try to sprint toward it, his front legs surging ahead while his back ones stumbled, his body uncoordinated and fragile. It was both beautiful and heartbreaking, because even when his body failed him, his will to live — to play — never wavered. However, as the weeks passed, the bad days began to outnumber the good.

He started to drag his back feet, first just one, then both. He'd stumble, fall, and look back at me in confusion — as if his body had betrayed him and he couldn't understand why. I tried to help him up, but each time I touched his sides, he'd yelp in pain. His strength had faded; his balance was gone. He wanted to go outside, but couldn't do it on his own. I began carrying him out like a child, holding his back end up in a wheelbarrow position so he could relieve himself without falling.

Even the wheelchair I'd ordered — the one I hoped would give him some freedom — seemed to bring him more discomfort than relief. He panted and shook when he was strapped into it, the tension in his body saying what words never could: this hurts.

By the end of that week, he was completely paralyzed in both hind legs. He could no longer stand. The pain was constant and unpredictable — sometimes sharp, other times dull but unrelenting. We were giving him all the medications we had — prednisone, gabapentin, amantadine, vetmedin — the full cocktail meant to ease inflammation, soothe nerve pain, and support his heart. But even those weren't enough anymore.

One night, I woke to the sound of a whimper. Clark had somehow tried to move from his bed beside mine, dragging himself into the living room before collapsing midway. I found him lying there, eyes wide with fear and confusion, unable to get up. I knelt beside him and whispered his name, pressing my forehead against his as I lifted him back into bed. His body was trembling. My heart broke in a way I didn't think it could again.

That night, I stayed on the floor with him — one arm wrapped around his chest, feeling every uneven breath. I stroked his fur, breathing in his scent, memorizing the rhythm of his heartbeat. I knew deep down that this was the beginning of the end. Still, a part of me hoped. Hoped that by morning he'd somehow be better, that the meds would kick in, that his body would give him one more miracle.

Morning came, and nothing changed. He lay beneath my wife's desk — his favorite safe space — trembling. He couldn't lift his head without wincing. His eyes, once full of mischief and light, now held only fatigue and pain. I went to work that day, checking my phone every few minutes, my wife sending me gentle updates from home. He wasn't improving.

When I came home that evening, I knew it was time to face what we had both been avoiding. Clark was still trying to hold his bladder, refusing to soil himself even though he hadn't urinated in over twenty-four hours. That was so him — proud, stubborn, dignified to the end. I carried him outside and put him in his wheelchair, his legs hanging limp beneath him, and as soon as he felt the cool air, he finally let go. It was like he'd been waiting — holding on until he could do it his way, on his terms.

Afterward, we sat together on the porch. The air was cool and quiet, the kind of fall evening Clark used to love. I wrapped my arms around him, running my fingers through his fur, tracing the familiar lines of his face. My wife sat beside us, tears falling quietly as we talked — not just about what needed to be done, but about all the years that led us here. Every stick, every hike, every snowball, every toss of the frisbee, every night he'd rested his head on my chest. Clark watched us both, his eyes soft but steady, and I swear he knew. He looked at my wife — not me — with this deep, knowing stare, as if to say, help him do what he can't bring himself to do.

We called the vet.

We wanted to do it at home, in the place he loved most, but no one nearby offered that service. So, with his blanket and favorite toy, we carried him to the clinic. He rested his head in my arms the entire way, calm and quiet — like he understood that this was his final ride.

The staff at the vet's office were incredible. They cleared a quiet room, dimmed the lights, and laid a soft blanket on the floor. They explained each step with gentle clarity — how the sedation would help him relax first, how the euthanasia medication would follow, how it was completely painless. It was comforting to hear that, to know that what we were doing wasn't to take life away but to take the pain away.

Euthanasia — from the Greek eu (good) and thanatos (death) — literally means "good death." It's a word that carries so much weight, yet so much mercy. When done right, it allows a dog to drift peacefully out of suffering, surrounded by love and familiarity. For dogs like Clark, who had given everything, it's the final act of compassion — not about giving up, but about letting go.

I carried him into the room and laid with him on the blanket. I ran my hands through his fur, memorizing every texture, every mark. His breathing was ragged; his body, tense. The vet came in softly and gave him the first injection — a sedative to calm him, to ease him into rest. Within moments, his muscles loosened. His breathing slowed. And for the first time in six long weeks, he truly relaxed.

He grumbled — that same low, throaty sound I called his "horn" — a sound that meant I'm here, I'm safe, I love you. Then, with a long sigh, he let go of the tension he'd been carrying. His body softened, his breathing evened out, and as the sedative took full effect, he finally released his bladder — the last physical thing he'd been holding onto.

I kissed his head over and over, whispering how much I loved him, thanking him for every single moment we'd shared. After what felt like forever, the vet gently administered the final injection. I held Clark close as I felt his heartbeat slow beneath my hand — strong, steady, then faint, then still.

And just like that, the world went quiet.

He was gone.

For a moment, I just sat there in the silence, my hand still on his chest, half-expecting it to rise again. The stillness was unbearable, but it was also peaceful — because I knew he wasn't in pain anymore. He had fought long and hard, and he had done it with grace.

As I sat there, tears soaking into his fur, I realized something: letting him go wasn't about losing him. It was about keeping my promise — the hardest promise I'd ever make — to protect him, even from his own suffering.

Reflection

They say that love is measured not by how we hold on, but by how we let go. In that moment, I finally understood what that meant. Clark had spent his whole life being my protector — guarding the house, watching the family, standing between me and the world when I couldn't stand for myself. On that final day, it was my turn to protect him.

He came into my life when I was lost and taught me how to live again. And when he left, he taught me how to love beyond the boundaries of life itself. His body may have failed him, but his spirit never did. Even now, I still feel him — in the quiet moments, in the echo of a bark down the road, in the warmth that settles over me when I least expect it.

Clark didn't just change my life; he shaped it.

And in that final act of love, he showed me that some promises — even the hardest ones — are the truest expressions of devotion.

Chapter 10: The Quiet After

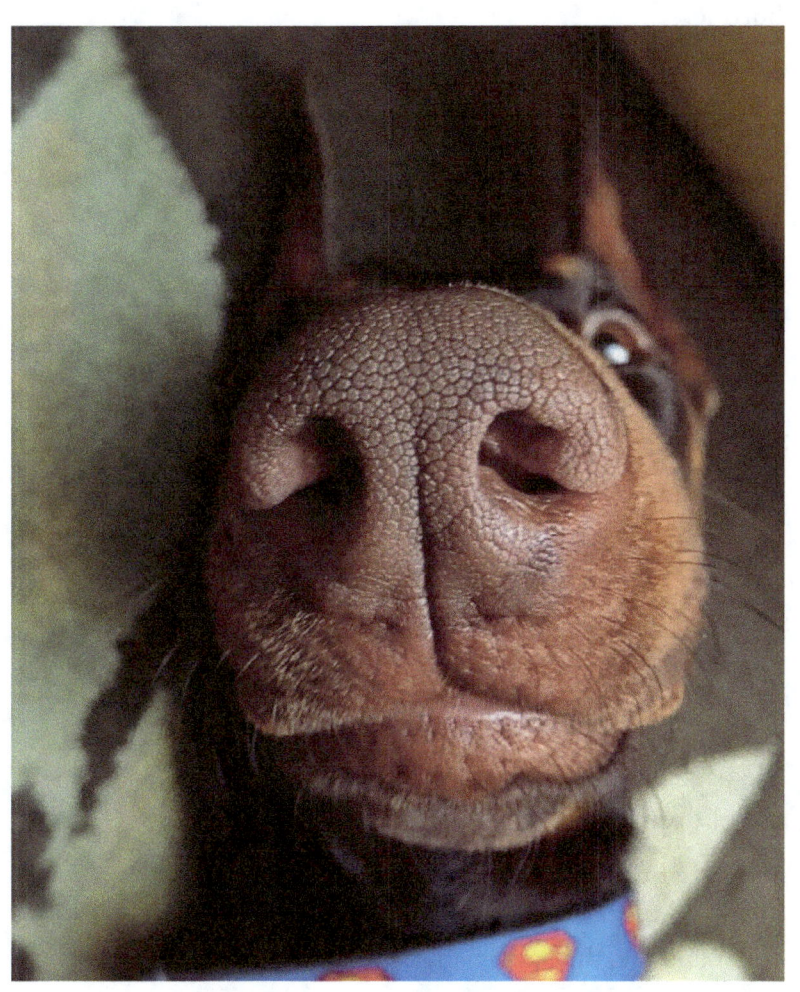

All I can think is that this has to be a dream. It can't be real.

I've lost my best friend.

We've lost a family member — and a part of us will always be hurting.

The house feels foreign now, quiet in a way that doesn't feel peaceful. We come home, and something is missing. The patter of his toenails across the floor. The soft "horn" he'd let out when he wanted attention. The constant, comforting presence of my shadow — that Velcro closeness every Doberman owner knows — is gone.

His pacing back and forth with nervous energy, his hopeful eyes waiting for the next round of fetch, the sound of his bark echoing through the yard — all gone. Even his watchful stance from the doorway, head held high, scanning for anything that didn't belong — gone. The space where he stood now just hums with silence.

We decided to have him cremated, so we could keep him with us forever.

When I got the call that his ashes were ready, I gathered every piece of his life I still had: his puppy paperwork, his first collar and tag, the small baby teeth I'd saved years ago. I wasn't ready for the weight of the box they handed me — how something that once bounded through our house could now fit in my hands. Yet, when I held him again, I felt peace. He was home.

That night, I went through every photo I could find — the ones friends and family had sent, and the hundreds on my phone. Looking back, I saw what I couldn't see in real time: the quiet shift in his eyes. After his injury, his expression had changed — a little sadder, a little more tired. He had probably been in pain longer than we ever realized. We just couldn't see it, because we were living it with him, one day at a time.

Now, the little reminders are everywhere. His hair still clings to the couch and his crate. I still catch myself stepping over the spot where his bed used to be. His last set of pawprints in the yard, pressed into the soft dirt — I can't bring myself to let the rain wash them away. Even his last pile of sticks by the fence line feels sacred now, like a monument to the joy he found in such simple things.

At dinnertime, the emptiness hits hardest. My wife still prepares the dogs' food with care, but there's always one bowl too many. The sound of Xena and Abbie trading bowls feels incomplete without Clark's big frame nudging between them, as if supervising the operation. The rhythm of our evenings is the same — but without his heartbeat in it.

I've seen a lot of loss in my life, but nothing compares to this. The grief that comes from losing a dog like Clark isn't just sadness — it's disorientation. He wasn't just part of our life; he shaped it. Every habit, every joy, every quiet moment had his mark on it. He's in the rhythm of the morning, the shadow of the porch, the air itself.

Still, I remind myself that love like his doesn't disappear.

It transforms.

The pain I feel is the echo of that love — and that means he's still here.

Writing this memoir, telling his story, has helped me heal in ways I didn't expect. Putting his life into words makes me feel close to him again — like we're still side by side, taking one last long walk together. Every memory brings both tears and laughter, and somehow, both feel right.

Clark was well-known in our little world — friends, family, neighbors. Everyone loved him. He never met a stranger, and if you met him once, you never forgot him. He had that rare soul that drew people in — strong, loyal, and full of love.

Picking up his ashes was the hardest step, but also the most comforting. When I carried him to the car, I could feel his presence again. Quiet. Warm. Home.

We'll keep him with Pete and Mr. Kitty — all waiting for us in their perfect forms somewhere beyond this life, chasing sticks, sunbathing, and keeping watch like they always have over the rainbow bridge.

And as strange as it sounds, I've started to feel lighter.

Not because I miss him any less, but because I understand now that grief is just love trying to find a place to rest.

Clark taught me how to live in the moment.

He taught me how to love unconditionally.

And now, he's teaching me how to let go — not in forgetting, but in continuing.

Because though he's gone, his lessons live on in me.

In how I love my family.

In how I show up for others.

And in how I find joy again, even in the quiet after

Epilogue: A Pawprint on My Heart

From the moment Clark picked me to be his dad, my life was never the same. He came barreling into my world at six weeks old — all clumsy paws and too-big ears — and somehow, he knew I needed him before I ever did. He saw something in me that I couldn't see in myself yet: someone worth loving, someone who could heal.

Clark wasn't just my dog. He was my constant, my shadow, my teacher. He was there through the darkest nights and the brightest mornings. He was the steady heartbeat that kept time with my own, the soul that made even ordinary days feel like they meant something.

He loved his family with every ounce of his being — always alert, always watching, always making sure everyone was safe. Whether he was proudly carrying a stick twice his size or curling up on the couch just to be touching someone, he lived every second with purpose. He was gentle when he could've been rough, loyal when the world felt uncertain, and brave even when his body began to fail him.

When his spinal condition took away his strength, it never took away his spirit.

Even in his final days, he faced life with that same stubborn heart — never growling, never snapping, even when he hurt. He just kept loving. That's who Clark was: all love, all heart.

We did our best for him in the end — carried him out to feel the sun on his face, held him close when the pain was too much. And when the time came to say goodbye, I whispered in his ear how much I loved him, how proud I was of him, and how thankful I was that he chose me.

Clark left this world with his head in my hands, surrounded by the people who loved him most. In that moment, I realized that the only thing stronger than grief is gratitude — gratitude for every tail wag, every muddy pawprint, every day we got to call him ours.

His spirit is still here — in the quiet corners of our home, in the rhythm of our days, in the way Xena tilts her head when she hears a sound outside. Clark taught me that love doesn't end when a heartbeat stops. It just changes shape.

So this isn't really goodbye. It's just "see you soon."

Until that day, I'll carry his pawprint on my heart — a mark that will never fade.

About

A true story of loyalty, loss, and love that sticks.

When Adam Lee Meade brought home a red rust Doberman puppy named Clark, he had no idea that this spirited, loyal, and deeply intuitive dog would become his compass through life's darkest and brightest seasons. Together, they navigated heartbreak, healing, laughter, and loss — a journey that revealed the unbreakable bond between humans and dogs.

Told with raw honesty and deep affection, *Clark: The Velcro Dog That Stuck to My Heart* captures what it truly means to be chosen by a dog. It is a tribute to every dog that never knew how to give space, and to every human who's glad they didn't.

Acknowledgments

To my wife, my family, and every friend who loved Clark as their own — thank you.

Your love, strength, and compassion carried us through the hardest moments.

And to Clark — you were more than a dog. You were family, a healer, and a reflection of all that's good in this world.

About the Author

Adam Lee Meade is a Family Nurse Practitioner, entrepreneur, and lifelong dog lover based in Fayetteville, West Virginia.

His bond with his Doberman, Clark, inspired this heartfelt memoir — a story of love, loyalty, and healing through companionship.

When not writing, Adam spends his time exploring the outdoors, helping others through his medical practice, and building ventures that bring people and purpose together.